SELLERS

PUBLISHING

Beads & Buttons

40 Jewelry & Accessory Projects

by Juliette Pettit

with Katia Feder

Published by Sellers Publishing, Inc.
161 John Roberts Rd.
South Portland, Maine 04106
For ordering information:
(800) 625-3386 toll free
Visit our Web site: www.rsvp.com • E-mail: rsp@rsvp.com

President & Publisher: Ronnie Sellers
Publishing Director: Robin Haywood
Managing Editor: Mary Baldwin
Senior Editor: Megan Hiller
Assistant Production Editor: Charlotte Smith
Photography: Claire Curt
Stylist: Charlotte Vannier
English translation: Roland Glasser
Additional crafts (pp. 18-19, pp. 42-43, pp. 54-55, and pp. 68-69)
  provided by Katia Feder; photography by Sophie Boussahba

ISBN 13:978-1-56906-988-2
LOC: 2007935162

Printed in China

10 9 8 7 6 5 4 3 2 1

Contents

Introduction

Anyone can make these forty handcrafted jewelry and accessory projects featuring beads and buttons. Use easy-to-find materials, some you likely already have on hand, to create a whole range of fun and original accessories.

Before beginning the projects in this book, search your drawers and storage bins for salvaged buttons, scraps of material from old clothes, leftover beads and other bits from past projects, and discarded jewelry for crafting items to reuse here. Search flea markets and thrift shops to increase your collection of recycled materials. Then dig in to these projects to discover what incredible new treasures you can create.

This book will teach you to use simple techniques in combination with everyday craft items to make bracelets, necklaces, rings, brooches, and bags with ease and style.

For My Little Treasure

YOU WILL NEED:

- a length of ribbon embroidered with the child's name
- a tape measure
- scissors
- round-nose pliers

- a large silver-plated metal ring
- a purple mother-of-pearl heart-shaped sequin
- a little plain mother-of-pearl star-shaped button

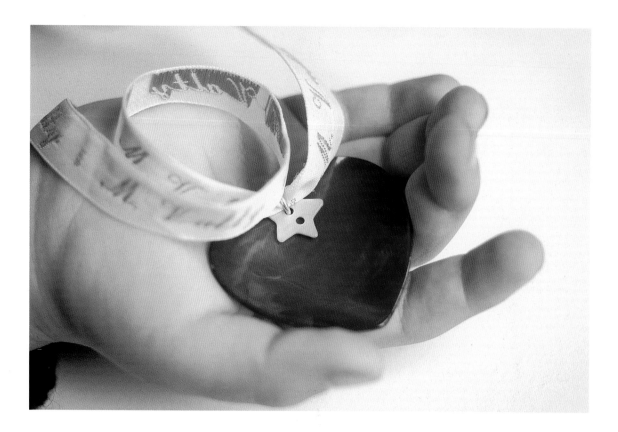

1. Cut a 10-inch-long piece of embroidered ribbon. **2. Use** the pliers to open the ring, string the heart-shaped sequin and the star-shaped button onto the ring, and close the ring securely again. **3. Pull** the length of ribbon half way through the ring to finish. Tie the small bracelet around the child's wrist.

Crocheted Wire Necklace

YOU WILL NEED:

- silver-plated metal wire
- a crochet needle
- a tape measure
- assorted mother-of-pearl buttons
- wire cutters
- little crimp beads
- flat-nose pliers
- a three strand clasp

1. Take the silver-plated metal wire and make a series of slip stitches to a length of approximately 2⅓ inches. **2. Pass** one of the loops of this metal-wire chain through one of the buttonholes of a button and crochet through this loop again to fix the button to the chain. Make another section of slip stitches then attach another button to the chain. Repeat this process until you have reached a length of about 20 inches. Cut the metal wire. Make two other chains of the same length, also decorated with buttons. **3. Use** crimp beads to fix the ends of the chains to the clasp.

Pretty in Pink

YOU WILL NEED:

- pink, mauve and purple seed beads
- thin metal wire (such as beading wire)
- tube beads
- 1 brooch pin (1¼ inches long)
- black cable wire
- a tape measure
- scissors
- little crimp beads
- flat-nose pliers
- wire cutters
- little purple pebble beads (both opaque and translucent)
- small mother-of-pearl buttons

1. String 12 pink beads onto a long piece of thin metal wire. Twist the wire on itself at the base of the beads to form a loop. Repeat twice more to make a set of three petals. **2. String** 18 mauve beads onto the same length of metal wire and twist the wire around the heart of the flower. Make two other mauve petals, twisting the wire round the center each time. Continue to make petals in the same way, increasing the number of beads for each successive row: Row three: 32 purple beads per petal. Row four: 24 tube beads per petal. Row five: 27 tube beads per petal. Row six: 30 tube beads per petal. Row seven: 32 tube beads per petal. **3. Attach** the brooch pin underneath the flower by passing the same piece of metal wire through the holes in the pin. **4. Cut** three 8-inch lengths of black cabled yarn and fold them in two. Pass them through the hole in the center of the brooch pin and use crimp beads to fix them together on top of each other. **5. String** pebble beads onto the ends, fixing each one in place with a single crimp bead. String on a few buttons and close each end with a single crimp bead.

Denim Flower

YOU WILL NEED:

- remnants of dyed plum-colored denim
- white seamstress chalk
- scissors
- remnants of cotton fabric with a flower print
- decorative scissors
- plum-colored cotton thread
- a needle
- 1 square mother-of-pearl button
- seed beads
- nylon thread
- little crimp beads
- flat-nose pliers
- tube beads
- 1 brooch pin (1¼ inches long)

1. Take a piece of plum-colored denim and use the seamstress chalk to draw a five-petal flower on it. Cut another flower from the same fabric, but slightly smaller, followed by a third a little smaller, and a fourth even smaller. **2. Take** the cotton flower-print fabric, cut a disc from it the same diameter as the smallest of the flowers and cut round its edge with the decorative scissors. Place the successive layers on top of each other, with the petals arranged in a staggered manner, and attach them by sewing them together in the middle with the button. Sew seed beads all around the edge of the button. **3. Take** a length of nylon thread, place a crimp bead at one of its ends, then string one tube bead and 30 seed beads onto the thread. Use the needle to pass the thread through one of the buttonholes and bring it back out the front of the button through the other hole. String 30 seed beads and one tube bead onto the thread and place one crimp bead after the last bead. Sew the brooch pin to the back of the flower.

Dancing Girl Brooch

YOU WILL NEED:

- thin metal wire
- wire cutters
- round-nose pliers
- 2 round frosted beads (8 mm in diameter)
- a round frosted bead (6 mm in diameter)
- 2 multifaceted crystal beads (8 mm in diameter)
- a green fancy bead
- 6 inches of coppered chain
- a round frosted bead (8 mm in diameter)
- a little gilded bead cap
- matte seed beads
- tube beads
- coppered jump rings (5 mm diameter)
- coppered kilt pin with 7 stationary loops

1. Take a short length of thin metal wire and use the round-nose pliers to make a loop in one end. String a bead onto it and close it in place with another loop. Use this procedure to string the 6 beads listed in the materials. **2. Cut** 6 pieces of chain of differing lengths and hook one bead setup onto each of them. Set them aside until you are ready to attach everything to the pin. **3. To make** the little girl: String one frosted bead, the cup bead, and one seed bead into the middle of 8 inches of thin metal wire. Using the seed bead as the end bead, thread the one end of the wire back through the cup bead and the frosted bead. Leave enough wire on each side to make two arms. String 3 or 4 tube beads followed by a seed bead on each arm wire. Again, use the seed bead as the end bead and rethread the remaining wire back through the last tube bead. Trim off any excess wire. **4. The dress** is a little triangle of woven seed beads. Fold 20 inches of wire in half. Begin the weave by stringing one bead into  the center of the 20 inches. Cross the wires and add 2 beads to make the next row. Continue to cross the wires and add beads, increasing the number of beads on each line. Each row of beads will have wires through it in each direction. The last line should have 10 beads strung on it. **5. Making** the legs: Rethread the wires part way through the longest row of beads so that the wires are coming out the bottom in a centered spot. String a few tube beads onto each of these two lengths of wire. Rethread each length of wire through the second to last bead and then cut it off. **6. Link** the head and body together. Use the jump rings to mount the chains and the girl to the kilt pin.

My New Bag

YOU WILL NEED:

- a handbag with wooden handles
- white wool fabric (to replace handbag's existing fabric)
- scissors
- plum-colored cotton thread
- white cotton thread
- a needle
- mother-of-pearl and shell buttons
- seed beads
- tube beads
- glass beads
- sewing machine
- hemp twine
- an upholstery needle
- 34 inches of plum-colored velvet ribbon (1 inch wide)

1. Remove the fabric from your bag and use the shape as a pattern to cut out a piece from the white wool fabric. Use the plum-colored cotton thread and the needle to sew the buttons onto the fabric in little flower patterns (*see photo*). Then take the seed beads, the tube beads, and the glass beads, and use the same needle and thread to sew star and flower motifs onto the fabric. Make a firm knot at the beginning and end of each little group of beads — that way if a thread breaks you will lose only some of the beads, not all of them. **2. Fold** the wool fabric in two, right sides together, and sew the two short sides together with the sewing machine. **3. Turn** the bag inside out and attach the upper edges of the bag to the wooden handles using the hemp twine and the upholstery needle. Pass the ribbon through the notches in the handles and sew the ends together with the plum-colored thread, making a 1-inch fold.

Cozy Necklace

YOU WILL NEED:

- multicolored looped wool
- a crochet needle
- a tape measure
- scissors
- mother-of-pearl buttons of different sizes and colors
- nylon thread
- little crimp beads
- a crimp tube clasp
- flat-nose pliers

1. Take the wool and make slip stitches using the crochet needle, leaving approximately 10 inches of unstitched wool at the start. Crochet the wool to a length of approximately 12½ inches. Leave another 10 inches of unstitched wool and cut the wool from the ball. **2. Repeat** the procedure twice and plait together the three unstitched threads at each end. Attach the buttons to the wool necklace using a piece of nylon thread that you pass through each button, binding them tightly to the necklace by placing crimp beads on the back of the necklace. **3. Place** the buttons across the whole necklace in an irregular fashion, varying the colors and the shapes. Fold the plaited threads of wool in half at a distance of ⅓ of an inch from the start and place the crimp tube clasp around them. Use the flat-nose pliers to crimp the clasp shut and cut off any excess wool.

Even Cozier Necklace

YOU WILL NEED:

- several colored decorative buttons
- crocheted wool flowers
- silver-plated fine metal wire
- wire cutters
- red, pink, and mauve seed beads
- assorted colors of cotton thread
- a needle
- plum-colored velvet ribbon (¾ inch wide)
- scissors
- a tape measure
- a snap

1. Attach a button to the center of each of the wool flowers, using a small piece of silver-plated metal wire. Embroider the beads around the edges of the flowers, varying the colors with the assorted cotton thread. **2. Cut** a length of 15 inches from the plum-colored velvet ribbon and sew the flowers to it in a regularly spaced manner. **3. Turn** up a ½ inch wide edge at each end of the ribbon and sew it using tightly spaced small stitches. Attach the snap with a few stitches.

Odds and Ends Bracelet

YOU WILL NEED:

- a mini-drill and drill bits
- 8 buttons of the same color but different sizes
- thin silver-plated metal wire
- wire cutters

- pebble beads
- large round beads
- silver-plated jump rings
- a clasp
- flat-nose pliers

1. Use the mini-drill to place two holes opposite each other 2 mm from the edge on each button. Use the thin metal wire to fix one large bead or one pebble bead into the center of each button. **2. Twist** the metal wire on itself behind each button and pass the ends through the holes so that you won't prick yourself. **3. Assemble** the bracelet by linking the buttons together with the silver-plated rings and use the flat-nose pliers to close the clasp.

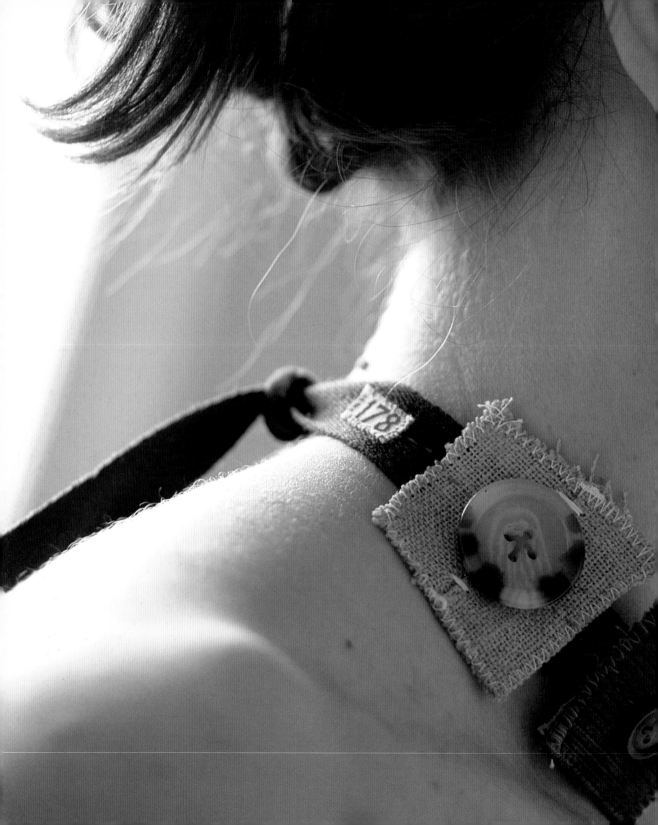

Sampler Necklace

YOU WILL NEED:

- small pieces of linen-twine fabric, boiled wool, and corduroy
- a tape measure
- cotton thread: fuchsia and cream-colored
- a needle
- scissors
- buttons in various sizes made of mother-of-pearl, horn, and light-colored wood
- herringbone ribbon
- a fabric label with embroidered number

1. Cut out 2-inch squares from the various fabrics. Whip stitch the four sides of each square to prevent fraying, using the fuchsia-colored thread for some and the cream-colored thread for others. **2. Sew** a button into the middle of each one using the fuchsia-colored thread. **3. Center** and sew these squares onto the ribbon: pass the thread through the buttons and sew a running stitch along the length of the ribbon. **4. Use** the same thread to sew the number label to the ribbon using gros point stitches. To wear, tie the necklace off at desired length.

Leather Button Bracelet

YOU WILL NEED:

- velvet ribbon (¾ of an inch wide)
- scissors
- a tape measure
- 4 leather buttons of different sizes
- matching cotton thread
- a needle
- 1 snap or Velcro closure

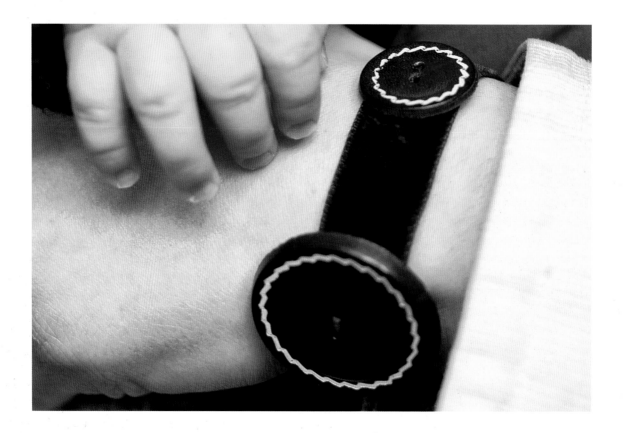

1. Cut a 9-inch length of velvet ribbon and sew the buttons onto it at irregular intervals. **2. Make** a double hem ⅓ of an inch long underneath each end of the ribbon and use petit-point stitches to hold it in place. **3. Sew** the two halves of the snap (or Velcro closure) to each end of the bracelet to make the closure.

Corduroy Flower

YOU WILL NEED:

- brown corduroy fabric
- a tape measure
- scissors
- a needle
- brown cotton thread

- a large horn button
- 5 little mother-of-pearl buttons
- blue and mauve seed beads
- 1 brooch pin (1¼ inches long)

1. Cut five discs (1¾ inches in diameter) from the corduroy. Arrange them into a flower shape and sew them firmly together with the brown cotton thread. **2. Sew** on the central button, followed by the little mother-of-pearl buttons around it. Stitch the blue and mauve beads into the fabric and in a cluster through the buttonholes. **3. Sew** the pin to the back of the brooch.

Personalized Bracelet

YOU WILL NEED:

- a piece of ribbon (grosgrain or velvet, ½ an inch wide)
- a tape measure
- scissors
- matching stranded cotton thread
- 9-hole buttons
- an embroidery needle

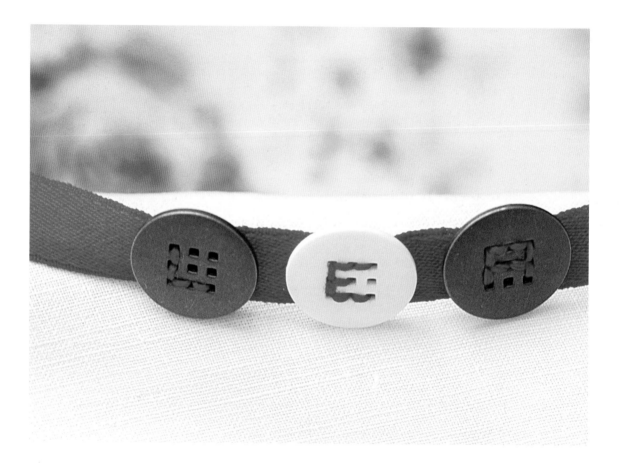

1. Cut a 12-inch length of ribbon. Embroider the buttons with your name, using a back stitch, fixing them to the ribbon as you do so. **2. Start** with the middle letter of the name, making sure that it is placed in the middle of the ribbon. The bracelet simply ties around the wrist.

Buttons Galore

YOU WILL NEED:

- cotton cord in a variety of colors
- a tape measure
- scissors
- 40 (approximate) buttons of varying sizes and colors
- large glass beads

1. Cut four lengths of 20 inches and two lengths of 28 inches from the various cords. String the buttons onto them, making a simple knot at the back of each button and placing them 1½ to 2 inches apart. **2. It is** important to place them on the cords in an irregular manner so that they do not cover each other once you have finished the bracelet. String all the large glass beads in one location onto one of the cords in between two buttons. Leave a 4-inch stretch free of buttons at the end of each cord. Link all of the cords together by making a knot 2⅓ inches from the end of the shorter cords and 6⅓ inches from the ends of the longer ones. Tie the cords together in this manner on both ends. **3. Take** the two longest cords at each end and wind one around the ends of the remaining cords (approximately five times) so as to hold them all together. Make a double knot with the other long cord. **4. Tie** the longest two ends in a bow at your desired length. This piece may be worn either as a necklace or a bracelet.

Sea Anemone Ring

YOU WILL NEED:

- fine nylon thread
- scissors
- 30 (approximate) white frosted drop beads (4 x 6 mm in size) drilled through at top and bottom
- 30 (approximate) matte brown seed beads
- a copper-plated metal ring finding mounted with a flat pierced open-work setting

For the alternative piece:
- fine nylon thread
- scissors
- 6 green drop beads (6 x 9 mm in size) drilled through at the top point
- a brass-plated metal ring finding mounted with a pierced open-work setting
- a rhinestone (8 mm in diameter)
- a gilded perforated claw setting for a rhinestone (8 mm in diameter)
- gem glue

1. Using approximately 1 yard of nylon thread, pass the thread successively through the base of one drop bead, one seed bead, then double back through the drop bead. **2. Attach** each bead to the ring base by passing the thread through a perforation. **3. Bring** the thread up through the next perforation and add another bead set. Continue in this way, ensuring that the beads are packed tightly together. Secure the final bead set by bringing the thread down through an opening in the setting and knotting it tightly.

Variant: flower with green drop beads **1. String** the six drop beads onto the nylon thread to form a six-petal flower. Pass the ends of the thread though the beads twice and bring them out at two opposite points. **2. Attach** the flower securely to the ring base with the nylon thread, making several knots. **3. Place** the rhinestone in the setting and close the claws. To attach the rhinestone setting to the ring, pass two lengths of nylon thread through the perforations of the settings, then under the ring. Secure the setting in place with several knots and a spot of glue.

Charmed, I'm Sure

YOU WILL NEED:

(Not all of these items are required for one bracelet. These materials are for different methods of making this charm bracelet. Read the complete directions to determine exactly which materials you will require.)

- silver-plated metal chain with large links
- fancy buttons (various shapes, colors, sizes)
- silver-plated metal jump rings (¼ inch in diameter)
- silver-plated metal hooks
- round-nose pliers
- fancy charms and sequins
- beading wire
- wire cutters
- small crimp beads
- flat-nose pliers
- silver-colored seed beads
- nylon thread
- a clasp
- a tape measure

1. Hang the fancy buttons onto your chain using the silver-plated metal jump rings or hooks. Use the round-nose pliers to open a jump ring slightly, slip the ring through the button hole, slip the ring through a link in the chain, then close the ring to secure all. If the button is too thick to hold both the button and the link to the chain, add a second jump ring to allow some dangle. Use the same technique to hang the charms and sequins between them. You may also replace each jump ring or hook with a small length of beading wire held in place with a crimp bead. For this method, insert a small crimp bead onto each wire,

string the button or charm onto the wire, loop the wire back through the chain then back on itself, pulling it through the crimp bead every time it passes it. Use the flat-nose pliers to crimp the bead closed and use the wire cutters to trim any excess wire. **2. If you** do not have a chain then make one using the seed beads: take one long piece of nylon thread and fold it in half. String 10 seed beads onto the folded nylon threads, then pass the two excess threads through the hole of the last bead, crossing them as you do so. **3. String** four beads onto one of the nylon threads and six beads onto the other one. Pass the thread bearing the smaller number of beads through the hole of the sixth bead on the other thread, crossing them again. Continue in this way until you have created a chain that is about 7 inches long. **4. Use** a single small crimp bead to close the chain. Use the silver-plated jump rings to attach the clasp onto the bracelet, then hang as many buttons and charms on it as you wish, using the technique described previously.

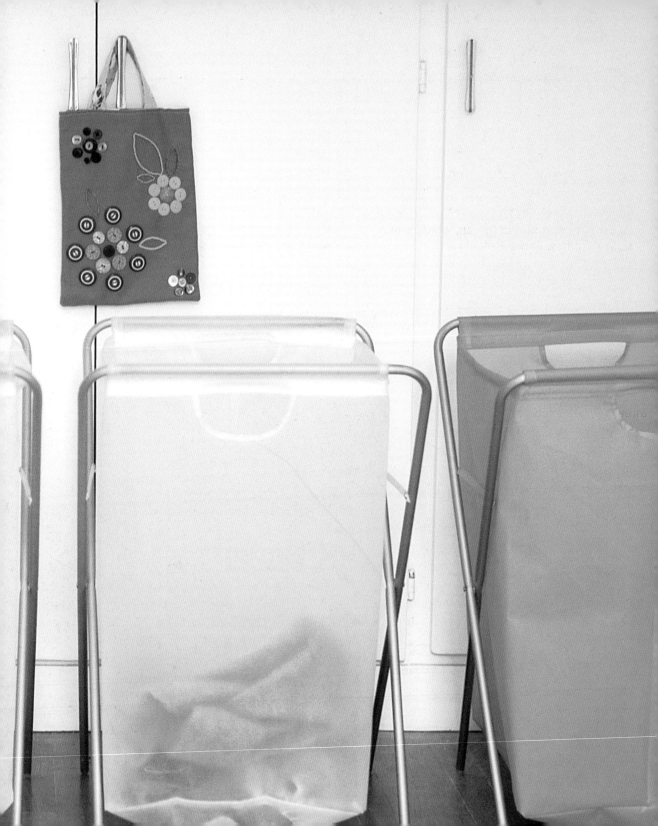

Spring Fling Bag

YOU WILL NEED:

- green cotton fabric (8 x 20 inches)
- polka-dot cotton fabric (15 x 10 ½ inches)
- flower-print cotton fabric (2 strips 13⅓ x 2⅓)
- a sewing machine
- fancy buttons in different colors and sizes
- assorted cotton thread (green, white, pink, purple, yellow, and sky blue)
- a needle
- seed beads (blue, green, pink, yellow and mauve)
- scissors
- a tape measure
- an iron
- pins
- white seamstress chalk

1. **Overcast** all of the pieces of fabric on a sewing machine to prevent fraying. Fold the rectangle of green fabric in two lengthways and sew buttons onto one of the halves of the piece of fabric using the cotton thread. 2. **Embroider** the petals using the seed beads, stitching three or four of them together at a time. Make sure that you leave at least 1½ inches of free space around each of the motifs, so that they do not crowd each other. Fold the two halves of the green fabric right sides together and machine stitch the two sides together ⅓ of an inch from the edge, then turn right side out. 3. **Fold** the polka-dot fabric in two, right sides together, stitch the long side ⅓ of an inch from the edge but do not turn it inside out. 4. **To make** the handles: make a hem ⅛ of an inch wide on each of the long sides of the two strips of flower print materials and fold each of the rectangles in two width-ways with right sides together. 5. **Mark** the pleats with an iron and machine stitch the strips of fabric ¹⁄₁₆ of an inch from the edge on the two long sides. Turn right side out

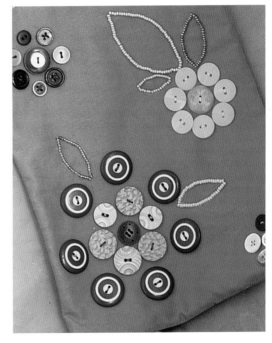

and pin the handles to each exterior side of the bag face to face and then slip the polka-dot bag over the green one. Pin and machine stitch both bags together ¾ of an inch from the edge at the open end of the green bag. 6. **Turn** the polka-dot bag inside out and make a ⅓ of an inch hem at the bottom of the bag. Machine stitch ¹⁄₁₆ of an inch from the edge then slip the polka-dot bag into the green bag.

Lucky Charm Necklace

YOU WILL NEED:

- iron
- a 2½-inch square of thick fabric
- nylon thread
- 7 navy blue buttons (½ inch in diameter)
- white and navy-blue cotton thread
- a navy-blue button (¾ inch in diameter)
- black, green, and pearly-white seed beads
- scissors
- a needle
- small crimp beads
- flat-nose pliers
- a clasp (springring, lobster, or box)
- a 2¼-inch square of black felt
- fabric glue

1. **Use** the iron and press to make a hem ⅓ of an inch wide around the edge of the square of fabric and secure the hem using a few tack stitches. Sew the small buttons onto the center of the square of fabric using the navy-blue thread, placing them in a circle. 2. **Now** sew the large button into the center of the circle. Sew the pearly-white seed beads around the button flower, using the white cotton thread. 3. **Cut** a 20½-inch length of nylon thread and use the needle to thread it into the hem underneath the square of fabric. Center the square on the nylon thread and string black and green seed beads onto it, creating patterns of color. String one crimp bead onto each end of the nylon thread and pass the thread back through the crimp beads. 4. **Crimp** the beads firmly with the flat-nose pliers, leaving the excess nylon threads to form two small loops. Attach the clasp to these loops. Use the fabric glue to attach the black felt square to the back of the square of fabric.

Just the Right Touch

YOU WILL NEED:

- nylon thread (for the necklace and bracelet)
- cable wire (for the belt)
- a tape measure
- scissors
- wire cutters

- little crimp beads
- flat-nose pliers
- little seed beads
- fancy buttons in different colors and sizes

1. Use the wire cutters to cut 6-inch lengths of nylon thread or cable wire. Take one of these lengths and fix a crimp bead to one of its ends. String onto it seed beads of the same color to a length of about 2 inches. **2. Pass** the thread or wire through a crimp bead, through the hole of a button, then through the crimp bead again. Crimp the bead shut using the flat-nose pliers. Take another length of  thread or yarn and string a crimp bead onto it. Pass the thread through the button and then back through the crimp bead. **3. Crimp** the bead shut and string seed beads of the same color onto it to a length of about 4 inches. String one crimp bead onto the thread. Pass it through the hole of another button, then again through the crimp bead and crimp it shut. **4. Continue** in this way until the necklace is about 40 inches long and the belt 47 inches long. Make several such lengths for the necklace and tie a single length around your wrist for a bracelet.

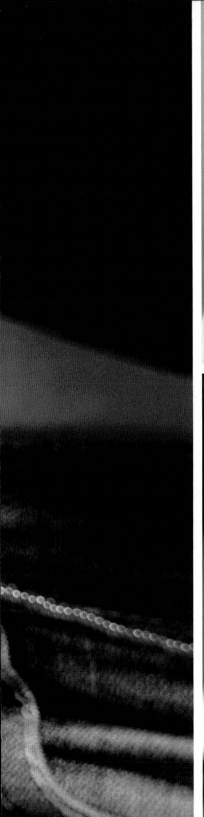
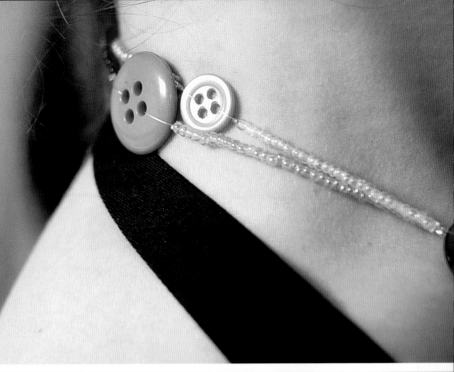

Glacier Necklace

YOU WILL NEED:

- 27½ inches of tubular metal ribbon
- 15 light-blue and mauve multifaceted crystal beads (8 mm in diameter)
- 9 transparent drop beads with top wires (4 x 6 mm)
- pliers
- 2 fold-over ends
- spring ring or lobster claw clasp
- jump rings

1. Insert the crystal beads into the tubular ribbon, spacing them out a little. Twist the ribbon between each bead. **2. Using** the pliers, carefully loop each drop bead's top wire around a bit of twisted ribbon between the crystal beads in the center of the necklace (see photo). **3. Finish** by attaching a fold-over end to each end of the ribbon and close with the pliers. Attach end to the clasp, using jump rings.

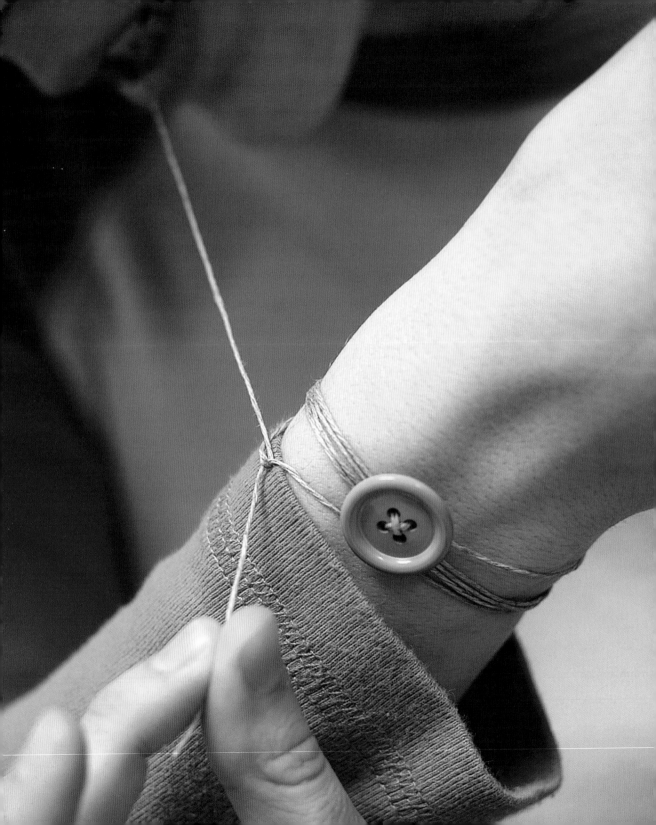

One-Button Bracelet

YOU WILL NEED:

- hemp string
- a tape measure
- scissors
- a medium to large button

1. Cut a 20-inch length of hemp string. Thread the string through the buttonholes several times so that it is pulled tightly into place. **2. Wind** the string around your wrist several times and knot it, centering the button above the middle of your hand.

On Edge

YOU WILL NEED:

- cable wire
- wire cutters
- a tape measure
- little crimp beads
- flat-nose pliers

- medium and long tube beads
- large seed beads
- fancy buttons in different colors and sizes
- clasps
- silver-plated jump rings

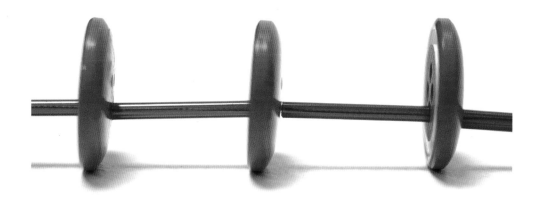

1. Cut 20-inch lengths from the cable wire for the necklaces and 10-inch lengths for the bracelet. String a single crimp bead onto one of the ends of each length and fold it back on itself for about ¾ of an inch by passing the cable wire back through the crimp bead. **2. Crimp** this bead shut, letting the cable wire form a little loop. String on tube beads, large seed beads and buttons, alternating them to create a regular pattern. **3. Complete** the necklaces and bracelet as you started them, by using a crimp bead to form a little loop in the cable wire. Use the jump rings to fix the clasps to the ends.

Super Rings

YOU WILL NEED:

For the satellite ring you will need:
- nylon thread
- scissors
- a nine-hole button
- seed beads of various sizes
- little crimp beads
- flat-nose pliers
- a fancy button

- an embroidery needle
- a flat ring support
- epoxy glue
- wooden craft stick

For the stack ring you will need:
- fancy buttons of various sizes and colors
- epoxy glue
- a flat ring support

Satellite ring: 1. Cut small lengths of nylon thread and pass the ends of each strand through the holes of the nine-hole button so that the ends are on the topside of the button. String a seed bead sandwiched between 2 crimp beads onto the top end of each of the 18 strands. Crimp the two crimp beads in place with the pliers to hold the decoration at the end of each strand. **2. Center** the fancy button on top of the nine-hole button, fanning the beaded strands around the edge. Attach the fancy button to the nine-hole button by sewing them together with more nylon thread and the embroidery needle. Make a double knot on the top of the fancy button, leaving small lengths of nylon thread coming out of the top. Bead these fancy threads as you did before, with a seed bead sandwiched between 2 crimp beads. **3. Glue** the fancy button onto the nine-hole button with the epoxy glue, spreading the glue in a thin layer with the craft stick. Leave it to dry, then glue the whole piece onto the ring support with the epoxy glue.

Stack ring: 1. Choose a range of buttons in contrasted colors and sizes and glue them together from largest to smallest, using the epoxy glue. **2. Glue** the piece onto the ring support using the epoxy glue.

One-Color Collection

YOU WILL NEED:

- fancy buttons of different sizes but the same general color
- mini-drill and drill bits
- silver-plated jump rings
- wire cutters
- 1 crimp clasp
- ribbon (to match the button color)
- scissors
- a tape measure
- flat-nose pliers

1. Lay your buttons out on your work surface and use the mini-drill to make holes in their edges so that you may link them together using the jump rings. Depending on how you link the buttons together you will need to make two or three holes in each button (see photo). Also make holes in the edges of the buttons placed at the extreme left and right of the necklace; these will allow you to attach jump rings to each one, through which you can pass the ribbon of the neck-

lace. **2. Link** the buttons together with the jump rings. Use the wire cutters to remove the fixture of the tube crimp clasp and pass a 13-inch length of ribbon through one of the rings situated at the end of the necklace. **3. Fold** the ribbon in two and fix it right next to the ring by crimping shut the tube crimp clasp using the flat-nose pliers. **4. Continue** at the other end of the necklace and fold the ends of the ribbons back on themselves several times to make them ¾ of an inch shorter — you will end up with a thick end to the ribbon, which will hold it in place in the flat crimp clasp. Fix the flat crimp clasp using the flat-nose pliers.

Button Brooch with Ribbons

YOU WILL NEED:

- 8 inches each of 6 kinds of ribbon of different widths, colors, and materials
- a needle and thread
- matte finish olive-green mother-of-pearl 4-hole button (1½ inches in diameter)
- thin nylon thread
- 6 amethyst-colored spinning-top crystal beads
- scissors
- a brooch pin
- glue (optional)

1. Fold one ribbon back on itself to form a kind of loop in the center of which the button will sit. Attach the ribbon to the button with a few stitches. Attach the second ribbon diagonally in the same way. Place each of the remaining ribbons in the same way, with equal spacing between each one, so that their colors and positions are balanced. **2. Bring** a piece of nylon thread up through one buttonhole and string two beads onto it, then pull the thread through the opposite buttonhole to attach them to the center of the button. **3. Pull** the same nylon thread up through a different buttonhole and string 4 beads onto it. Then bring the thread through the final hole and tighten it to secure all beads to the top center of the button. **4. Finish** by sewing or gluing the brooch pin to the back of the brooch.

Flash Your Pearly Whites

YOU WILL NEED:

- a tape measure
- grosgrain ribbon (1 inch wide)
- matching cotton thread
- a needle
- small mother-of-pearl buttons
- a metal hook clasp
- heat-seal paper
- cotton ribbon of the same color and width as the grosgrain ribbon
- scissors
- iron

1. Measure the circumference of your neck using the tape measure and add ¾ inch to this length. Sew the mother-of-pearl buttons next to each other onto the grosgrain ribbon, making sure that they are properly aligned. **2. Leave** a margin of ⅓ inch at the beginning and end of the ribbon. When you have covered the entire length of the ribbon, sew each half of the metal hook clasp to each end of the ribbon (⅓ inch from the end). Turn the margins back over the clasp halves and sew them using large stitches. **3. Cut** off a strip of heat-seal paper, as well as a length of matching cotton ribbon, to the same size as the collar. Apply the strip of heat-seal paper to the underside of the collar using an iron on the linen setting (usually the highest temperature setting) but no steam. Remove the protective strip from the heat-seal paper and fix the cotton ribbon to it, still using the iron. The same technique is used to make the bracelet, but it is quicker!

Just Splendid

YOU WILL NEED:

- a mini-drill and drill bits
- a red mother-of-pearl button (37 mm in diameter)
- 7 natural mother-of-pearl buttons (22 mm in diameter)
- 6 red mother-of-pearl buttons (22 mm in diameter)
- 2 pink square mother-of-pearl buttons (15 mm on each side)
- 2 pink square mother-of-pearl buttons (10 mm on each side)
- 2 natural mother-of-pearl flower buttons (17 mm in diameter)
- 2 natural mother-of-pearl flower buttons (10 mm in diameter)
- 3 pink mother-of-pearl buttons (15 mm in diameter)
- 2 natural mother-of-pearl buttons (15 mm in diameter)
- silver-plated metal wire
- wire cutters
- 14 silver-plated jump rings (8 mm in diameter)
- round-nose pliers
- 2 pink cotton cords (8½ to 9 inches each)
- 2 small silver-plated crimp beads
- 2 silver-plated cord ends
- flat-nose pliers
- a silver-plated clasp

1. Use the mini-drill to make two holes in the following buttons: the very large red button, the natural mother-of-pearl buttons (22 mm in diameter), and the red mother-of-pearl buttons (22 mm in diameter). Place the holes opposite each other, 2 mm from the edge. **2. Using** the photo above as inspiration, place the remaining various buttons on top of each other and fix them together by passing the silver-plated metal wire through their holes three times. Twist the wire around itself at the back of the buttons and poke the remaining ends through the buttonholes. **3. Using** the round-nose pliers, gently open the jump rings, link all of the button combinations together, closing the jump rings as you go. **4. Take** the pink cords and pass one through each of the rings on the ends of the necklace. Fold each cord in two and slip a small crimp bead onto each one. Place the small crimp bead immediately after the jump ring attached to the top of the last button. Use the flat-nose pliers to crimp the beads. Place a cord end onto the other end of each doubled cord. Attach the cord ends to the ends of the cords using the flat-nose pliers. Attach the cord ends to the clasp.

Mermaid Necklace

YOU WILL NEED:

- plain cotton cord
- a tape measure
- scissors
- approximately 35 natural mother-of-pearl buttons (1 inch in diameter)
- 1 pale blue mother-of-pearl button (1 inch in diameter)
- 1 pale blue mother-of-pearl button (1½ inches in diameter)
- 1 light green mother-of-pearl button (1½ inches in diameter)
- 1 red mother-of-pearl button (½ an inch in diameter)
- 1 plain mother-of-pearl button (½ an inch in diameter)

1. Cut four 20-inch lengths and two 28-inch lengths of cord. String buttons onto each of them, fixing them in place just by knotting the cord at the back, and spacing them 1¼, 1½, or 2 inches apart. Save the small, plain mother-of-pearl button to finish the necklace. **2. The reason** for spacing the buttons irregularly is so that they do not cover each other once the necklace is finished. Leave four inches free of buttons at each end of the cords. **3. Link** all of the cords together by making a knot 2⅓ inches from the ends of the shorter lengths and 6¼ inches from the ends of the longer ones. **4. Fold** back the two ends of one of the longer cords to make two loops and pass the little plain mother-of-pearl button (½ an inch in diameter) through one of them. **5. Use** the second long cord to tie the groups of cords together tightly, from the knot to the loop. Close the necklace with a double knot.

Delightful Rings

YOU WILL NEED:

For a flat ring you will need:

- brushed metal spacers that could be used for necklaces and bracelets
- wire cutters
- epoxy resin
- mother-of-pearl buttons (1 inch in diameter approximately)
- mother-of-pearl buttons (¼ of an inch in diameter approximately)
- 1 flat metal ring support

For a charm ring you will need:

- 1 silver-plated metal ring support with jump rings
- mother-of-pearl buttons (¼ of an inch in diameter approximately)
- mother-of-pearl buttons (⅓ of an inch in diameter approximately)
- glass pebble beads
- silver-plated metal wire with end-pieces
- flat-nose pliers

Flat ring

1. Use the wire cutters to cut the brushed metal spacers to remove the clasps and resize to fit the buttons. **2. Use** the epoxy resin to attach the spacer to the large button and one small button in the center of the spacer. Leave to dry flat, then glue the whole piece onto the ring support.

Charm ring

1. Use the silver-plated jump rings to fix the buttons to the ring support. **2. String** the pebble beads onto the metal wire and fix them onto the ring support by using the flat-nose pliers to make a closed loop.

Dangling Buttons Necklace

YOU WILL NEED:

- a silver-plated metal choker
- thin metal wire (pink and gray)
- nylon thread
- crimp beads
- 4 mother-of-pearl buttons in different colors approximately ¾-inch diameter
- 8 mother-of-pearl buttons in different colors approximately 1 to 1¼ inches in diameter
- wire cutters
- flat-nose pliers
- scissors

1. Wrap the choker with pink metal wire for 1¼ inches. With the wire cutters trim so the point end will not be against your skin. Then, attach one nylon thread, blocking it in place on the choker with a single crimp bead. **2. String** one mother-of-pearl button onto this thread and block it in place with a single crimp bead. Pass another thread through the second button-hole and block it in place with a crimp bead. **3. Continue** in this way until you have attached three buttons in a line. Make four equal lengths and space them 1¼ inches apart on the choker. **4. Wrap** the free spaces on the choker with alternating colors of metal wire.

Mother-of-Pearl Choker

YOU WILL NEED:

- a silvered metal choker
- fine navy-blue metal wire (approximately 28 gauge)
- a tape measure
- wire cutters
- very fine beading wire (.012, 49-strand)
- crimp beads

- flat-nose pliers
- little translucent light-blue and navy-blue tube beads
- oval translucent glass beads
- mother-of-pearl buttons in different sizes, shapes, and colors

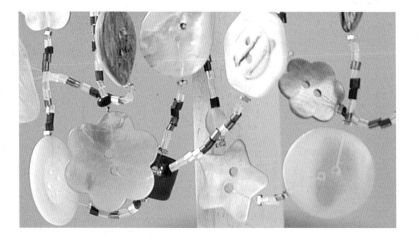

1. Wrap the metal choker with the navy-blue wire to cover approximately ⅓ inch worth of the choker. Trim the wire at the end of the wrap so that the point end will not be against your skin. **2. Take** a length of the very fine beading wire, make a tight loop around the choker at the point where you stopped wrapping the metal wire, and use a crimp bead to crimp it in place. String several beads, a crimp bead, and a mother-of-pearl button onto this length of wire. Pull the wire through one of the buttonholes then double-back through the crimp bead, and crimp it closed. Pass another piece of wire through the second hole of the button and block it with a crimp bead. String several more beads onto the thread, then attach the thread to another button using a crimp bead. Continue in this way until you have reached a total length of around 6 inches. Use another crimp bead to attach the end of this string of beads and buttons to the metal choker. Make five such strings of beads and buttons and attach them all to the metal choker in an overlapping fashion. **3. Leave** about 1 inch between each attachment point. Wrap the bare choker between these points with the navy-blue wire as you did in the first step. Add final ⅓ inch of navy-blue wire to complete the piece.

Mother-of-Pearl Brooches

YOU WILL NEED:

- several sizes of mother-of-pearl buttons
- brooch pins of the same widths as the buttons
- matching cotton embroidery floss
- an embroidery needle
- scissors

1. **Use** the embroidery floss and an embroidery needle to sew the buttons to the brooch pins. Pass the floss through the buttonholes several times and tighten well. Finish by making a double knot on the back of each pin.

A Bag that Measures Up

YOU WILL NEED:

- light-brown linen (7¾ x 20½ inches)
- mauve cotton fabric (15 x 10⅓ inches)
- a sewing machine
- 36 assorted mother-of-pearl buttons
- a needle
- assorted cotton thread (light-brown, mauve, brown, and white)
- scissors
- a tape measure
- brown ribbon (1 inch wide)
- pins
- woven tape measure (or ribbon printed with numbers)
- white seamstress chalk

1. Overcast all of the pieces of fabric on a sewing machine to prevent fraying. **2. Fold** the linen rectangle in two lengthways and sew 35 buttons onto one half of it using the light-brown cotton thread. Arrange the buttons in horizontal and vertical lines leaving a 1⅓-inch margin around the edges. Cut 4 inches of brown ribbon and sew the last button onto it 1⅓ inches from the right-hand side. Fold the ribbon in half (keeping the button on top) and pin it to the side of the linen bag, lining it up with the edge and 1¼ inches from the top opening. **3. Fold** the piece of linen in two, right sides together, then pin the two halves together. Machine stitch the left and right-hand sides together ⅓ of an inch from the edge, then turn right side out. Fold the mauve fabric, right sides together, in half and stitch the long side ⅓ of an inch from the edge, but do not turn it right side out. **4. Cut** a 13¾ inch length from the brown ribbon and another identical length from the woven tape measure. Machine stitch the woven tape measure to the brown ribbon in such a way that it runs down the middle widthways. Pin the ribbons flat to each outside of the bag, facing each other, and pull the mauve bag over the linen bag. **5. With** the mauve bag inside out, slip it over the brown one. Pin the two bags together and machine stitch them ¾ of an inch from the open end of the brown bag. Turn the mauve bag right side out and make a ⅓ of an inch hem along the bottom of the bag. Machine stitch it 1/16 of an inch from the edge then insert the mauve bag into the brown linen one.

Little Flowers

YOU WILL NEED:

- a pink mother-of-pearl button (1 inch wide)
- an embroidered flower on thick canvas
- 5 heart-shaped natural mother-of-pearl buttons
- pink cotton thread
- a needle
- nylon thread
- little crimp beads
- 2 pebble beads
- mauve metallic tube beads
- mauve and pink seed beads
- flat-nose pliers
- a brooch pin (1 inch wide)
- scissors

1. Sew the pink button onto the center of the flower and the heart-shaped buttons onto the petals, using the pink cotton thread. String one crimp bead, one pebble bead, and about seven tube beads onto the nylon thread. **2. Pass** the nylon thread through the eye of the needle and sew through the central button. Bring the nylon thread out of the front of the flower through the other buttonhole and string about 7 tube beads, 1 pebble bead, and 1 crimp bead onto it. Crimp the crimp beads closed with the flat-nose pliers. **3. Take** another length of nylon thread and repeat the operation, this time replacing the tube beads and pebble beads with the mauve and pink seed beads. Sew the brooch pin onto the back of the flower, using the pink cotton thread.

Seed Beads and a Button Bracelet

YOU WILL NEED:

- 8 (12-inch) lengths of beading wire
- a 2-hole mother-of-pearl button (35 mm or 1¼ inches in diameter)
- thin transparent tape
- seed beads
- 2 jump rings
- a split ring
- a clasp
- 14 crimp beads
- flat-nose pliers
- wire cutters

1. Pass all seven lengths of beading wire up through one of the button holes and back down through the other. Center the button in the middle of the wires and put a piece of tape to one side to prevent the button from moving along the wires. **2. Beginning** on the side of the button without the tape, fill the seven lengths of wire with seed beads until you have covered enough to wrap halfway around your wrist with the button centered in the top. (Note that the clasp and rings will add approximately ¾ of an inch to the final length of the bracelet.) There should be excess wire after the final bead. Place a piece of tape at the end of each

beaded strand to hold it until you are ready to crimp. **3. Remove** the tape from the side of the centered button and fill those seven lengths of wire with seed beads until it matches the opposite side. Tape each strand as you complete it to make sure the beads do not slide off. To make sure the beaded wires (on both sides) are equal in length, you can either count the number of beads (use approximately 50 per strand per side if using 8/0 seed beads) or measure the beaded strand (between 3 and 4 inches, depending on your wrist circumference if using smaller or mixed-size seed beads). **4. Attach** a jump ring to the clasp. On one side of the bracelet, remove the tape from one of the strands and pass the end of the beaded wire strand through a crimp bead, then through the jump ring attached to the clasp, then back through the crimp bead to form a small loop. Make sure to push all the beads tightly toward the center of the bracelet, then use the flat-nose pliers to tighten the crimp bead at the top of the beads leaving a small loop between the crimp bead and the jump ring so that the strands of beads can move slightly. Repeat this process until all seven beaded strands are attached to the jump ring and are crimped in place on this side of the bracelet. Attach the split ring to the second jump ring. Repeat the same crimping process on the other side of the bracelet, but pull each strand through a crimp bead, through a split ring, and back through the crimp bead before closing in the same manner. **5. To finish** the bracelet, thread about an inch of excess wire from each strand back through the beads, then use the wire cutters to clip off any remaining wire.

Shades of Blue Bracelet

YOU WILL NEED:

- navy-blue cotton fabric
- an embroidery frame
- blue grosgrain ribbon (1 inch wide)
- scissors
- a needle
- matching cotton thread
- seed beads
- 3 blue mother-of-pearl buttons (¾ inch diameter)
- navy-blue cotton ribbon
- a tape measure
- a white mother-of-pearl shoe button

1. Stretch a piece of navy-blue fabric over the embroidery frame. Cut a 7-inch piece from the grosgrain ribbon and baste the edges of the ribbon onto the stretched fabric. **2. Embroider** as many tight lines of beads as required to make a square. Leave an empty space of ¾ of an inch, then embroider another square of beads. **3. Continue** until you have embroidered four squares of beads, then sew the mother-of-pearl buttons into the empty spaces. Remove the stretched fabric from the frame and cut it at just over ½ inch from the edges of the ribbon. **4. Rebaste** the edges of the fabric under the ribbon and cut a 7-inch piece from the navy-blue cotton ribbon. Place this on the back of the grosgrain ribbon and sew them together along the edges using tight little stitches. **5. Turn** back ⅓ inch at each end of the two ribbons. To make the fastening: string seed beads onto a double length of cotton thread. Make a loop at one end and attach the shoe button at the other. **6. Finish** by making a double knot and passing the needle and thread through the thickness of the bracelet. Bring the needle and thread out 1½ inches farther and use the scissors to cut off the excess thread at the level of the fabric.

Spring Flower

YOU WILL NEED:

- white felt
- a soft pencil
- scissors
- white cotton thread
- a needle
- small pearly-white buttons
- beading wire (approx. 12 inches total)
- wire cutters
- seed beads in various colors
- small crimp beads
- flat-nose pliers
- fabric glue
- a 1¼-inch-long safety-pin base

1. Draw a flower shape (approximately 3½ inches across) on the white felt with the soft pencil. Place a second piece of felt underneath and cut both of the felt flower shapes out with the scissors. **2. Cover** one of the felt flowers entirely with buttons (by sewing them on). **3. Use** the tip of the scissors to make two small holes in the center of the flower. Cut three pieces of beading wire, each one measuring about 4 inches long. Pass the threads through the first hole in the flower and back out through the second. String the seed beads onto these threads, placing and crimping a crimp bead on each end to hold the seed beads in place. **4. Apply** the fabric glue to the back of the buttoned flower and stick the second felt flower to the back of it. Leave it to dry, then sew the safety-pin base onto the back of the flower.

Index

Acknowledgments

Thank you to Perles Box, Aventures créatives, Loisirs et Créations, LaCroix et la Manière, and Jeu de mailles for having supplied me with beads, buttons, and accessories to realize these designs.

Thank you to Perles Box, L'Entrée des fournisseurs, and Emmaüs for having given us the permission to take photographs in their shops.
Thank you to Cyrielle for her precious help.
Thank you to Tana publications and to Véronique.
Thank you to Claire for her photographs.
Thank you to Françoise and to Pascal for letting us invade their home.
Thank you to Olivia, Margot, Joséphine, Coco, Eugène, and Marcel for having endured the camera flashes.

Thank you to my pretty little bead and my two handsome buttons.